1.

- - 1

Summary..4

Chapter 2 7

Chapter 1: Understanding ADHD in Adult Men..........9

Chapter 2: The Impact of ADHD on Life 17

Chapter 3: Beyond Medication - A Holistic Approach to Managing Symptoms.............................26

Chapter 4: Embracing Self-Acceptance and Strengths 36

Chapter 5: Practical Survival Toolkit for Everyday Life 44

Chapter 6: Real-Life Anecdotes from Men with ADHD...53

Chapter 7: Navigating the Emotional Rollercoaster...62

Chapter 8: Building Supportive Relationships 71

Chapter 9: For Partners, Family Members, Friends, and Employers...80

Chapter 10: Thriving with ADHD in the Modern World...89

Chapter 11: Additional Resources for Further Exploration 98

Chapter 12: Overcoming Challenges in Daily Life with ADHD..107

Synopsis..116

2.
3.
4.
5.
6.
7.
8.
9.
10.
11.
12.
13.
14.
15.

16.

Summary

Chapter 1: Understanding ADHD in Adult Men

3

1.1 The Basics of ADHD

3

1.2 Debunking Myths and Misconceptions

5

1.3 Neurological Underpinnings and the Male Brain

6

Chapter 2: The Impact of ADHD on Life

8

2.1 Work and Career Challenges

8

2.2 Relationships and Social Interactions

10

2.3 Self-Esteem and Personal Identity

11

Chapter 3: Beyond Medication - A Holistic Approach to Managing Symptoms

13

3.1 Dietary Advice for ADHD Management

13

3.2 Exercise Routines Tailored for Hyperactivity

3.3 Cognitive Behavioral Techniques and Mindfulness Practices ... 15

Chapter 4: Embracing Self-Acceptance and Strengths ... 17

4.1 The Importance of Self-Acceptance ... 19

4.2 Harnessing Individual Strengths ... 19

4.3 Overcoming Challenges with Positivity ... 21

Chapter 5: Practical Survival Toolkit for Everyday Life ... 22

5.1 Time Management Strategies ... 24

5.2 Organizational Tips for Adults with ADHD ... 24

5.3 Maintaining Focus Amidst Distractions ... 26

Chapter 6: Real-Life Anecdotes from Men with ADHD ... 28

6.1 Stories of Struggle and Success — 30

6.2 Lessons Learned on the Journey with ADHD — 30

6.3 Inspiring Others Through Personal Experiences — 32

33

Chapter 7: Navigating the Emotional Rollercoaster

35

7.1 Dealing with Frustration and Low Self-Worth

35

7.2 Overcoming Social Stigma

37

7.3 Building Resilience

38

Chapter 8: Building Supportive Relationships

40

8.1 Improving Communication Skills

40

8.2 Finding Professional Help When Needed

42

8.3 Creating a Supportive Environment

44

Chapter 9: For Partners, Family Members, Friends, and Employers

46

9.1 Understanding ADHD in Adult Men

46

9.2 How to Offer Support

48

9.3 Encouraging Constructive Dialogue

50

Chapter 10: Thriving with ADHD in the Modern World

52

10.1 Redefining the Relationship with ADHD

52

10.2 Strategies for Success in Work and Life

54

10.3 Empowerment through Education

56

Chapter 11: Additional Resources for Further Exploration

58

11.1 Books, Websites, and Communities

58

Chapter 12: Overcoming Challenges in Daily Life with ADHD

64

12.1 Strategies for Managing Time and Priorities

64

12.2 Organization Techniques for Adults with ADHD

66

12.3 Coping with Distractions and Maintaining Focus

68

1

Understanding ADHD in Adult Men

1.1 The Basics of ADHD

The initial exploration into the realm of Attention Deficit Hyperactivity Disorder (ADHD) in adult men begins by demystifying the core aspects of this condition. Understanding ADHD is crucial, not only for those directly affected but also for society at large, to foster empathy and support. This section delves into the neurological basis of ADHD, highlighting how it diverges from common misconceptions and sheds light on its multifaceted impact on an individual's life.

At its core, ADHD is characterized by a pattern of inattention, hyperactivity, and impulsivity that is inconsistent with developmental expectations. However, what sets adult manifestations apart is how these symptoms adapt and present in mature scenarios such as the workplace or within relationships. For men especially, societal expectations often compound the challenges faced, making recognition and acceptance of the condition a pivotal first step.

Neurologically, ADHD involves an imbalance in neurotransmitter activity within the brain, affecting regions responsible for executive function—planning, decision-making, and impulse control. This imbalance is not a matter of willpower or motivation but rather a tangible divergence in brain function that requires understanding and appropriate management strategies.

- Debunking myths: Contrary to popular belief, ADHD goes beyond mere difficulty with concentration; it encompasses a broad spectrum of cognitive challenges and strengths.

- Impact on daily life: From professional achievements to personal relationships, ADHD influences various facets of life differently in men due to societal roles and expectations.

- Holistic management approaches: Effective management combines medication with behavioral strategies tailored to adult responsibilities and realities.

This foundational knowledge paves the way for deeper insights into managing ADHD effectively. By recognizing its neurological underpinnings and dispelling stereotypes, individuals can approach treatment with clarity. Moreover, understanding these basics encourages a shift from merely coping to thriving despite ADHD's challenges. Through comprehensive education on these fundamentals, men are better equipped to navigate their journey with ADHD confidently.

1.2 Debunking Myths and Misconceptions

The journey into understanding ADHD in adult men necessitates confronting and dismantling the myriad myths and misconceptions that cloud public perception. This step is vital not only for those directly experiencing ADHD but also for broader societal acceptance and support. By challenging these inaccuracies, we pave the way for a more informed and empathetic approach to managing ADHD.

One prevalent myth is that ADHD is exclusively a childhood disorder, implying that adults, particularly men, either outgrow it or never had it in the first place. This misconception overlooks the substantial body of research indicating that ADHD often persists into adulthood, with symptoms evolving rather than disappearing. For adult men, this evolution can mean less hyperactivity but more pronounced challenges with organization, time management, and emotional regulation.

Another common fallacy is the notion that ADHD is simply an excuse for laziness or lack of discipline. This belief fundamentally misunderstands the neurological underpinnings of ADHD as a disorder of executive function—affecting planning, focus, and impulse control—rather than a moral failing or character flaw. Men with ADHD may face additional stigma here due to societal expectations around masculinity and productivity, making it even more crucial to dispel this myth.

- ADHD symptoms in adults are often mislabeled as personal failings rather than recognized as manifestations of a neurological condition.
- The stereotype that men must always be in control and unemotional can prevent them from seeking help or acknowledging their struggles with ADHD.

- Misconceptions about treatment options can also hinder effective management; medication is frequently seen as the sole solution when in reality, a combination of medication, therapy, lifestyle adjustments, and coping strategies is often most beneficial.

In conclusion, debunking myths surrounding adult male ADHD is essential for fostering understanding and encouraging appropriate treatment approaches. By recognizing the complex reality of living with ADHD—as opposed to oversimplified stereotypes—we enable men to seek help without shame and society to offer support without judgment. This shift towards informed awareness lays the groundwork for improved quality of life for men with ADHD and their communities.

1.3 Neurological Underpinnings and the Male Brain

The exploration of ADHD in adult men requires a deep dive into the neurological underpinnings that characterize this condition, particularly as they manifest in the male brain. Understanding these foundations is crucial for demystifying ADHD and providing targeted support. The male brain, influenced by both biological and environmental factors, exhibits unique patterns that can affect the presentation and management of ADHD.

Research indicates that ADHD is linked to several key areas within the brain, including those responsible for executive functions such as planning, impulse control, and attention regulation. In males, differences in brain structure and activity have been observed when compared to females with ADHD, suggesting a gender-specific aspect to how symptoms manifest and impact daily functioning. For instance, studies have shown variations in the prefrontal cortex—an area critical for executive function—between genders, which may contribute to the differing symptomatology seen in men and women.

Moreover, neurotransmitter systems play a significant role in ADHD. Dopamine and norepinephrine are two neurotransmitters known to be involved in attention processes and motivational systems. Imbalances or dysfunctions within these systems are thought to contribute significantly to the symptoms of ADHD. Given that hormonal influences can modulate neurotransmitter systems differently in males versus females, this could further explain some of the gender-specific manifestations of ADHD.

- Men with ADHD might experience more pronounced issues with impulsivity and risk-taking behaviors due to these neurological differences.

- The societal expectation for men to exhibit control and emotional stoicism can exacerbate stress and anxiety among males with ADHD, potentially leading to underdiagnosis or misdiagnosis.

- Treatment approaches may need customization considering these neurological variances; what works well for women or children with ADHD might not be as effective for adult men.

In conclusion, delving into the neurological underpinnings specific to the male brain reveals significant insights into how ADHD manifests uniquely in men. This understanding not only challenges stereotypes but also opens avenues for more personalized treatment strategies that consider both biological differences and societal pressures faced by men with ADHD. By acknowledging these nuances, we move closer towards comprehensive care models that address individual needs effectively.

References:

- Seidman, L.J., Valera, E.M., & Makris, N. (2005). Structural brain imaging of attention-deficit/hyperactivity disorder. Biological Psychiatry, 57(11), 1263-1272.

- Rubia, K. (2018). Cognitive neuroscience of attention deficit hyperactivity disorder (ADHD) and its clinical translation. Frontiers in Human Neuroscience, 12, 100.

- Ivanchak, N., Fletcher, K., & Jaconis, M. (2011). Gender differences in adult attention-deficit/hyperactivity disorder: Results from a national sample. Journal of Clinical Psychiatry, 72(4), 463-469.

- Arnsten, A.F.T. (2009). Toward a new understanding of attention-deficit hyperactivity disorder pathophysiology: An important role for prefrontal cortex dysfunction. CNS Drugs, 23(Suppl 1), 33-41.

- Biederman, J., & Faraone, S.V. (2005). Attention-deficit hyperactivity disorder in adults: epidemiology, pathogenesis and treatment. Drugs Today (Barc), 41(9), 597-606.

2

The Impact of ADHD on Life

2.1 Work and Career Challenges

The intersection of ADHD and the workplace presents a unique set of challenges that can significantly impact an individual's professional life. For men with ADHD, navigating these challenges requires not only an understanding of their symptoms but also strategies to mitigate their effects in a work environment. This section delves into the specific hurdles faced by men with ADHD in their careers and offers insights into overcoming them.

One of the primary issues is maintaining focus and productivity in traditional office settings. Men with ADHD often find themselves struggling with prolonged attention to tasks, leading to underperformance or inconsistent work quality. The dynamic nature of ADHD means that while they may excel in creative problem-solving and high-energy tasks, routine and detail-oriented work can become sources of frustration.

- Difficulty adhering to structured schedules and meeting deadlines
- Challenges in organizing tasks or prioritizing workloads effectively
- Tendency towards procrastination, especially on complex or long-term projects

Beyond task-related challenges, interpersonal relationships at work can also be affected. Communication difficulties may arise from impulsivity or misunderstandings, potentially leading to conflicts with colleagues or supervisors. Moreover, the social aspects of the workplace, such as networking and teamwork, can be daunting for those who struggle with hyperactivity or attention regulation.

In conclusion, while men with ADHD face distinct challenges in the workplace, recognizing these issues is the first step towards crafting a fulfilling career path. By employing targeted strategies and advocating for necessary accommodations, individuals can harness their unique skills and thrive professionally despite the hurdles posed by ADHD.

To navigate these career obstacles, it's crucial for men with ADHD to leverage their strengths while seeking accommodations that align with their needs. Strategies such as using technology for organization, breaking down projects into manageable steps, and setting up regular check-ins for accountability can be beneficial. Additionally, fostering an open dialogue about ADHD with employers can lead to adjustments in work patterns or environments that better suit their cognitive style.

2.2 Relationships and Social Interactions

The realm of relationships and social interactions presents a complex landscape for individuals with ADHD, where the nuances of social cues and the demands of emotional regulation can pose significant challenges. This section explores how ADHD influences interpersonal dynamics, friendships, romantic relationships, and family life, offering insights into navigating these waters with greater awareness and understanding.

For many with ADHD, the core symptoms such as impulsivity, inattention, and hyperactivity can inadvertently affect their social interactions. Impulsivity may lead to interrupting others during conversations or making hasty decisions that impact relationships negatively. Inattention might manifest as difficulty maintaining focus during long conversations or forgetting important dates and commitments, which can be misconstrued as lack of interest or care. Hyperactivity can make calm, collected interactions challenging, potentially leading to restlessness in settings that require stillness or patience.

- Challenges in reading social cues and responding appropriately
- Difficulty maintaining long-term relationships due to inconsistent communication
- Struggles with emotional dysregulation impacting interpersonal conflicts

Beyond individual symptoms affecting behavior, the broader implications on one's social life are profound. Misunderstandings arising from missed cues or forgotten commitments can strain friendships and romantic partnerships. Moreover, the effort required to navigate these social complexities often leads to feelings of isolation or misunderstanding among those with ADHD.

To foster healthier relationships, it is crucial for individuals with ADHD to develop strategies tailored to their unique challenges. Open communication about one's needs and struggles can pave the way for understanding and support from friends, partners, and family members. Additionally, seeking professional guidance through therapy or coaching can equip individuals with tools for better emotional regulation and communication skills.

In conclusion, while ADHD poses distinct challenges in the realm of relationships and social interactions, recognizing these hurdles is a vital step towards building stronger connections. Through self-awareness, open dialogue, and targeted strategies for improvement, individuals with ADHD can enhance their relational well-being significantly.

2.3 Self-Esteem and Personal Identity

The intersection of self-esteem and personal identity forms a critical area of impact for individuals with ADHD, shaping their experiences and perceptions in profound ways. This section delves into how ADHD symptoms can influence one's sense of self-worth and identity, exploring the nuanced challenges faced by those affected. Understanding these aspects is crucial for fostering a supportive environment that nurtures positive self-perception and growth.

Individuals with ADHD often grapple with feelings of inadequacy and chronic underachievement due to the pervasive nature of their symptoms across various life domains. The constant struggle with inattention, impulsivity, and hyperactivity can lead to repeated failures or criticisms in academic, professional, and social settings. These experiences frequently translate into a negative self-image, where one's identity becomes intertwined with perceived failures or shortcomings.

The impact on self-esteem is further compounded by external misconceptions and stigma associated with ADHD. Misunderstandings about the condition can lead to labeling individuals as lazy or incapable, reinforcing internalized negative beliefs about oneself. This stigma not only affects personal identity but also hinders the pursuit of help or accommodations that could mitigate some of the challenges associated with ADHD.

- Challenges in academic achievement often leading to feelings of frustration and low self-worth
- Social difficulties stemming from impulsivity or misunderstanding social cues contributing to isolation or peer rejection
- Professional struggles due to inconsistent performance or organizational difficulties impacting career development

To counteract these effects on self-esteem and personal identity, it is essential for individuals with ADHD to engage in positive reinforcement strategies. Recognizing strengths, celebrating small victories, and setting realistic goals can help build a more positive self-image. Additionally, seeking support from therapists who specialize in ADHD can provide strategies for managing symptoms while fostering a healthier relationship with one's own identity.

In conclusion, navigating the complexities of self-esteem and personal identity requires an understanding approach that acknowledges the unique challenges posed by ADHD. By focusing on strengths, seeking appropriate support, and challenging societal stigmas, individuals with ADHD can cultivate a stronger sense of self-worth and a more resilient personal identity.

References:

- American Psychiatric Association. (2013). Diagnostic and Statistical Manual of Mental Disorders (5th ed.). Arlington, VA: American Psychiatric Publishing.
- Barkley, R. A. (2015). Attention-Deficit Hyperactivity Disorder: A Handbook for Diagnosis and Treatment (4th ed.). New York, NY: Guilford Press.
- DuPaul, G.J., & Stoner, G. (2014). ADHD in the Schools: Assessment and Intervention Strategies (3rd ed.). New York, NY: Guilford Press.
- Faraone, S.V., Asherson, P., Banaschewski, T., Biederman, J., Buitelaar, J.K., Ramos-Quiroga, J.A., Rohde, L.A., Sonuga-Barke, E.J.S., Tannock, R., &

Franke, B. (2015). Attention-deficit/hyperactivity disorder. Nature Reviews Disease Primers, 1(15020).

- Hallowell, E.M., & Ratey, J.J. (2011). Driven to Distraction (Revised): Recognizing and Coping with Attention Deficit Disorder from Childhood through Adulthood. New York: Anchor Books.

3

Beyond Medication - A Holistic Approach to Managing Symptoms

3.1 Dietary Advice for ADHD Management

The role of diet in managing Attention Deficit Hyperactivity Disorder (ADHD), especially in adult men, is a topic of increasing interest and research. Nutritional strategies can complement traditional treatments, offering a holistic approach to symptom management. This section delves into the specifics of dietary advice aimed at mitigating the symptoms of ADHD, exploring how certain foods and eating patterns can influence cognitive function and behavior.

Emerging evidence suggests that the brain's neurochemistry is not only affected by medication but also by the nutrients it receives from our diet. For individuals with ADHD, certain dietary adjustments have been shown to potentially reduce symptoms. These include:

- High-Protein Foods: Incorporating protein-rich foods such as lean meats, fish, eggs, beans, and nuts into meals can help improve concentration and possibly make ADHD medications work longer.

- Complex Carbohydrates: Eating complex carbohydrates like fruits, vegetables, and whole grains may aid in reducing the hyperactive component of ADHD and encourage a better sleep cycle.

- Omega-3 Fatty Acids: Found in fish such as salmon, tuna, and sardines as well as flaxseed and walnuts, omega-3 fatty acids are believed to play a crucial role in brain function and may decrease ADHD symptoms.

    Beyond specific nutrients, maintaining stable blood sugar levels through regular meal times can also significantly impact mood and attention spans. Skipping meals or relying on high-sugar snacks can exacerbate symptoms of hyperactivity and impulsiveness.

While these dietary recommendations offer potential benefits for managing ADHD symptoms, it's important to note that individual responses to dietary changes may vary. Therefore, any significant modifications should be undertaken with guidance from healthcare professionals who understand both nutrition and ADHD. Additionally, these dietary strategies should complement other treatment modalities like medication therapy or behavioral counseling rather than replace them.

In conclusion, adopting specific dietary practices may serve as an effective adjunct strategy for adults dealing with ADHD. By focusing on nutrient-rich foods that support brain health and stabilizing blood sugar levels through mindful eating patterns, individuals may experience an improvement in their ability to manage symptoms associated with ADHD.

3.2 Exercise Routines Tailored for Hyperactivity

The significance of exercise in managing hyperactivity, particularly within the context of Attention Deficit Hyperactivity Disorder (ADHD), cannot be overstated. This section delves into the development and implementation of exercise routines specifically designed to mitigate symptoms of hyperactivity, offering a complementary approach to traditional ADHD management strategies. The focus on physical activity as a therapeutic modality reflects a broader understanding of how structured movement can positively affect cognitive function, emotional regulation, and overall well-being.

Exercise routines tailored for individuals with hyperactivity are grounded in the principle that certain types of physical activity can have direct benefits on brain structure and function. These benefits include improvements in executive functioning, attentional control, and behavioral inhibition. Aerobic exercises such as running, swimming, cycling, and team sports are particularly effective due to their ability to increase heart rate and promote the release of endorphins and dopamine—neurotransmitters that play key roles in mood regulation and impulse control.

In addition to aerobic activities, mindfulness-based exercises like yoga and tai chi have shown promise in managing ADHD symptoms. These practices emphasize controlled movements, breathing techniques, and mental focus—all of which are beneficial for individuals struggling with hyperactivity and impulsivity. By incorporating these exercises into daily routines, individuals may experience not only reductions in hyperactive behaviors but also improvements in stress management and self-awareness.

- Aerobic Exercises: Activities that increase cardiovascular health while boosting mood-regulating neurotransmitters.
- Mindfulness-Based Practices: Exercises focusing on breath control, movement precision, and mental concentration to enhance emotional regulation.
- Structured Team Sports: Participating in team sports can provide social interaction and develop skills such as teamwork and discipline which are often challenging for those with ADHD.

In conclusion, integrating specialized exercise routines into the management plan for hyperactivity offers a holistic approach that extends beyond medication alone. By addressing physical health alongside cognitive and emotional needs through targeted physical activities, individuals with ADHD can achieve significant improvements in their symptoms and overall quality of life.

To maximize the benefits of exercise for managing hyperactivity, it is crucial that routines are consistent, enjoyable, and appropriately challenging. Tailoring activities to individual preferences ensures sustained engagement—a critical factor given the tendency towards novelty seeking among those with ADHD. Furthermore, setting realistic goals and gradually increasing intensity or complexity can help maintain motivation while preventing burnout or injury.

3.3 Cognitive Behavioral Techniques and Mindfulness Practices

The integration of cognitive behavioral techniques (CBT) and mindfulness practices into the management of various psychological conditions represents a significant advancement in therapeutic approaches. This section explores how these strategies, when combined, offer a powerful toolkit for individuals seeking to manage symptoms of anxiety, depression, ADHD, and other mental health issues. The emphasis on CBT and mindfulness underscores a holistic approach that goes beyond traditional medication, focusing on altering thought patterns and enhancing present-moment awareness.

Cognitive Behavioral Techniques are grounded in the concept that our thoughts, feelings, and behaviors are interconnected, and that modifying negative thought patterns can lead to changes in feelings and behaviors. CBT involves identifying specific challenges or triggers, understanding the negative thought processes that contribute to them, and then applying strategies to alter these thoughts and responses. Techniques such as journaling, role-playing, relaxation exercises, and structured problem-solving are often employed within CBT sessions to facilitate this process.

Mindfulness practices complement CBT by fostering an increased state of awareness of one's thoughts, emotions, and bodily sensations from moment to moment. Through practices such as meditation, mindful breathing, and yoga, individuals learn to observe their experiences without judgment. This heightened awareness can reduce the intensity of negative thoughts or feelings by creating a space between stimulus and response where choice lies. In essence, mindfulness offers a way to disengage from automatic negative thought spirals.

- Integration into Daily Life: Practical exercises from both CBT and mindfulness can be seamlessly integrated into daily routines. For instance, brief mindfulness meditations can help start the day with a sense of calmness while cognitive restructuring techniques can be used to tackle stressors as they arise.

- Enhanced Self-Regulation: Both approaches enhance emotional regulation skills. By understanding the nature of their thoughts and learning to stay anchored in the present moment, individuals can better manage emotional distress.

- Improved Resilience: Over time, consistent practice of CBT and mindfulness techniques builds resilience against future stressors by cultivating more adaptive coping mechanisms.

In conclusion, cognitive behavioral techniques combined with mindfulness practices offer a comprehensive approach for managing mental health symptoms. By addressing both the cognitive aspects through structured problem-solving and emotional regulation through present-moment awareness, individuals are equipped with effective tools for enhancing their well-being. As research continues to evolve in this area, it is clear that these strategies hold significant promise for those seeking alternatives or complements to medication-based treatments.

References:

- Hofmann, S. G., Asnaani, A., Vonk, I. J., Sawyer, A. T., & Fang, A. (2012). The Efficacy of Cognitive Behavioral Therapy: A Review of Meta-analyses. Cognitive Therapy and Research, 36(5), 427-440.

- Kabat-Zinn, J. (1994). Wherever You Go, There You Are: Mindfulness Meditation in Everyday Life. Hyperion.

- Segal, Z. V., Williams, J. M. G., & Teasdale, J. D. (2002). Mindfulness-Based Cognitive Therapy for Depression: A New Approach to Preventing Relapse. Guilford Press.

- Hölzel, B.K., Lazar, S.W., Gard, T., Schuman-Olivier, Z., Vago, D.R., & Ott U. (2011). How Does Mindfulness Meditation Work? Proposing Mechanisms of Action From a Conceptual and Neural

Perspective. Perspectives on Psychological Science, 6(6), 537-559.

4

Embracing Self-Acceptance and Strengths

4.1 The Importance of Self-Acceptance

The journey towards understanding and managing ADHD in adult men necessitates a foundational step of self-acceptance. This critical phase is not merely about acknowledging the presence of ADHD but embracing it as part of one's identity without judgment or self-reproach. Self-acceptance in this context serves as a powerful tool for transformation, enabling individuals to navigate their condition with resilience and optimism.

At its core, self-acceptance involves a deep recognition of one's strengths and limitations. For men with ADHD, this means understanding how their unique brain wiring contributes to both challenges and talents. It shifts the narrative from focusing solely on difficulties to recognizing the diverse abilities that ADHD can bestow, such as creativity, hyper-focus on passionate interests, and the capacity for out-of-the-box thinking.

Moreover, self-acceptance acts as a buffer against the stigma often associated with ADHD. By embracing their condition, men can challenge societal misconceptions and advocate for themselves in personal and professional settings. This proactive stance is crucial in fostering environments that support rather than hinder their progress.

- Building resilience through positive self-talk and reframing failures as learning opportunities.
- Enhancing relationships by communicating needs clearly and seeking understanding from others.
- Pursuing careers that align with their strengths, thereby increasing job satisfaction and performance.

In addition to personal growth, self-acceptance encourages the development of coping strategies tailored to individual needs. Recognizing one's specific ADHD-related challenges allows for a more targeted approach to management, whether through organizational tools, lifestyle adjustments, or seeking appropriate professional help.

Ultimately, the importance of self-acceptance lies in its ability to empower men with ADHD to lead fulfilling lives. By acknowledging their condition without shame or guilt, they can harness their unique strengths and navigate life's challenges more effectively. This foundational step paves the way for growth, success, and a deeper sense of well-being.

4.2 Harnessing Individual Strengths

The journey of self-acceptance for men with ADHD sets the stage for the pivotal next step: harnessing individual strengths. This phase is about moving beyond mere acceptance to actively leveraging one's unique abilities and talents. It involves a shift from understanding one's ADHD-related challenges to recognizing and utilizing the inherent strengths that come with this condition. The process of harnessing these strengths is not just beneficial but essential for personal and professional fulfillment.

Identifying one's strengths begins with introspection and may require feedback from trusted friends, family, or professionals who can provide objective insights. Men with ADHD often excel in areas requiring creativity, innovation, and the ability to think outside conventional frameworks. These attributes can lead to exceptional problem-solving skills, remarkable resilience in the face of challenges, and a unique perspective that can be invaluable in many settings.

- Exploring creative outlets that align with personal interests, such as art, music, or writing, where hyperfocus can lead to significant achievements.

- Seeking professions or roles that value innovative thinking and adaptability over rigid structures, thus capitalizing on natural inclinations towards dynamic environments.

- Utilizing their propensity for high energy levels in positions that require stamina and enthusiasm.

To effectively harness these strengths, it is crucial for individuals to develop strategies that mitigate the impact of ADHD symptoms on their daily lives. This might include organizational tools or techniques specifically designed to enhance focus and productivity. Moreover, establishing a supportive network—whether through professional mentors, peer groups focused on ADHD, or understanding friends and family—can provide encouragement and accountability.

In essence, harnessing individual strengths is about creating a life structure that accommodates ADHD while maximizing personal potential. It requires patience, self-awareness, and sometimes guidance from others but leads to a more authentic and fulfilling life path. By focusing on what they do best, men with ADHD can redefine their narrative from one of limitation to one of empowerment and success.

4.3 Overcoming Challenges with Positivity

The transition from harnessing individual strengths to overcoming challenges with positivity is a natural progression in the journey towards self-acceptance and empowerment for men with ADHD. This phase emphasizes the importance of maintaining a positive outlook in the face of adversity, which can significantly impact one's ability to navigate life's obstacles. The essence of this approach lies not in avoiding challenges but in transforming them into opportunities for growth and learning.

Adopting a positive mindset begins with acknowledging that challenges are an integral part of life, serving as catalysts for personal development and resilience building. It involves reframing negative experiences, focusing on solutions rather than problems, and cultivating gratitude for what one has achieved despite difficulties. This perspective shift enables individuals to view their ADHD-related challenges not as insurmountable barriers but as stepping stones towards achieving their goals.

- Practicing mindfulness and meditation to enhance emotional regulation and reduce impulsivity, thereby improving decision-making processes during challenging times.
- Setting realistic goals and celebrating small victories along the way to foster a sense of accomplishment and motivate further progress.
- Developing a support network of friends, family, and professionals who provide encouragement, advice, and constructive feedback when facing setbacks.

To effectively overcome challenges with positivity, it is crucial to develop coping strategies tailored to one's unique set of strengths and weaknesses. This might include time management techniques that accommodate periods of hyperfocus or distractibility, communication skills that help articulate needs or boundaries more clearly, or physical activities that channel excess energy productively. By leveraging these personalized strategies, men with ADHD can navigate their challenges more effectively while maintaining a positive outlook.

In conclusion, overcoming challenges with positivity is about embracing adversity as an opportunity for growth. It requires shifting one's perspective from viewing obstacles as limitations to seeing them as chances to leverage inherent strengths creatively. Through mindfulness practices, goal setting, building supportive networks, and employing individualized coping strategies, men with ADHD can cultivate resilience and achieve greater personal fulfillment.

References:

- Barkley, R. A. (2015). Attention-Deficit Hyperactivity Disorder: A Handbook for Diagnosis and Treatment. Guilford Publications.

- Hallowell, E. M., & Ratey, J. J. (2011). Driven to Distraction (Revised): Recognizing and Coping with Attention Deficit Disorder. Anchor Books.

- Seligman, M. E. P. (2006). Learned Optimism: How to Change Your Mind and Your Life. Vintage Books.

- Kabat-Zinn, J. (1994). Wherever You Go, There You Are: Mindfulness Meditation in Everyday Life. Hyperion.

- Duckworth, A. L. (2016). Grit: The Power of Passion and Perseverance. Scribner.

5

Practical Survival Toolkit for Everyday Life

5.1 Time Management Strategies

Effective time management is a cornerstone of navigating life with ADHD, especially for adult men who might face unique challenges in both professional and personal settings. This section delves into the importance of developing robust time management strategies that cater specifically to the needs of men with ADHD. By understanding and implementing these strategies, individuals can significantly improve their productivity, reduce stress, and enhance overall quality of life.

The first step in mastering time management is recognizing the value of structure. Men with ADHD often benefit from a predictable routine that minimizes uncertainty and reduces the likelihood of distractions.

Establishing a consistent daily schedule, including set times for work, exercise, meals, and relaxation, can provide a sense of stability and control.

- Prioritization: Learning to identify and focus on tasks that are most critical is crucial. Techniques such as the Eisenhower Box can help individuals distinguish between tasks based on urgency and importance.

- Breaking Tasks Down: Large projects can seem overwhelming for those with ADHD. Breaking them into smaller, manageable steps can make them seem more approachable and less daunting.

- Using Tools and Technology: Leveraging technology like smartphones or digital planners can be incredibly beneficial. Setting reminders for appointments, deadlines, or even short breaks can help keep one on track throughout the day.

- Limiting Distractions: Creating an environment conducive to focus is essential. This might mean decluttering a workspace or using apps that limit access to distracting websites or notifications during work hours.

In addition to these strategies, it's important for men with ADHD to cultivate patience and self-compassion. Progress may be gradual, and setbacks are part of the journey towards effective time management. Celebrating small victories along the way can boost morale and motivation.

Fostering accountability through partnerships or coaching can also play a pivotal role in improving time management skills. Whether it's a professional coach specialized in ADHD or a trusted friend committed to regular check-ins, having external support can provide additional motivation and insight.

In conclusion, while managing time effectively poses distinct challenges for adult men with ADHD, adopting tailored strategies can lead to significant improvements in both personal fulfillment and professional achievement. By embracing structure, utilizing tools wisely, minimizing distractions, and seeking support when needed, individuals can transform their relationship with time from one of struggle to one of empowerment.

5.2 Organizational Tips for Adults with ADHD

For adults with ADHD, organizational challenges can permeate every aspect of life, from the workplace to personal relationships. The essence of overcoming these hurdles lies in adopting tailored organizational strategies that cater to the unique needs and strengths of individuals with ADHD. This section explores practical tips and innovative approaches to organization that can significantly enhance daily functioning and overall well-being for adults living with ADHD.

The foundation of effective organization for adults with ADHD starts with simplification. Reducing clutter and minimizing possessions can decrease the amount of decision-making and maintenance required on a daily basis. This approach not only applies to physical spaces but also digital environments, where emails, notifications, and online distractions can overwhelm an already taxed attention span.

- Visual Organization Systems: Utilizing visual cues such as color-coded systems for filing documents or scheduling activities can be particularly beneficial. Visual aids serve as constant reminders and reduce the cognitive load associated with remembering tasks or locating items.

- Daily Planning Sessions: Spending a few minutes each morning to outline the day's priorities can help in maintaining focus on what truly matters. This practice allows for a structured approach to the day, accommodating both planned tasks and allowing flexibility for unexpected demands.

- Technology as an Ally: Leveraging technology through apps designed to aid in task management, time tracking, or habit formation can provide external support that compensates for executive function challenges common in ADHD.

- Routines Rooted in Personal Interests: Building routines around personal passions or interests ensures higher engagement levels. For instance, if someone enjoys music, incorporating it into cleaning routines can make the process more enjoyable and sustainable.

Incorporating these organizational strategies requires patience and self-compassion, recognizing that progress is incremental and setbacks are part of the learning curve. It's also crucial to celebrate small victories along the way, reinforcing positive behaviors and boosting motivation. Additionally, seeking support from professionals who understand ADHD can provide personalized strategies that resonate more deeply with an individual's specific challenges and lifestyle preferences.

In conclusion, while adults with ADHD may face distinct organizational challenges, embracing structured yet flexible strategies tailored to their unique needs can lead to significant improvements in managing daily tasks and enhancing overall quality of life. By prioritizing simplification, visual organization systems, strategic planning sessions, leveraging technology effectively, and aligning routines with personal interests, individuals can navigate their world with greater ease and confidence.

5.3 Maintaining Focus Amidst Distractions

In today's fast-paced world, the ability to maintain focus amidst a sea of distractions is more valuable than ever. This section delves into strategies and insights beyond traditional advice, offering a deeper understanding of how to cultivate a focused mindset in an environment that is constantly vying for our attention. The relevance of this topic extends from enhancing productivity to improving mental health, making it a critical component of the practical survival toolkit for everyday life.

The first step in maintaining focus amidst distractions is recognizing the sources of distraction and understanding their impact on our cognitive functions. Distractions can be external, such as social media notifications or background noise, or internal, like wandering thoughts or emotional turmoil. Acknowledging these distractions allows us to take proactive measures to minimize their influence.

- Creating a Conducive Environment: Tailoring your physical and digital workspace can significantly reduce external distractions. This might involve decluttering your desk, using noise-cancelling headphones, or employing website blockers during work hours.

- Mindfulness and Meditation: Cultivating mindfulness through meditation can enhance your ability to recognize when you're becoming distracted and gently guide your focus back to the task at hand. Regular practice strengthens the mind's focusing capabilities over time.

- Pomodoro Technique: Breaking work into short intervals (traditionally 25 minutes), followed by brief breaks, can help maintain high levels of focus while also providing necessary rest periods for your brain.
- Leveraging Peak Energy Times: Aligning challenging tasks with times of day when you naturally feel most energetic and alert can improve focus and efficiency.

Beyond these strategies, it's essential to cultivate an internal environment conducive to focus. This involves managing stress levels, ensuring adequate sleep, and maintaining a healthy dietâ€"all factors that significantly influence cognitive function and attention span. Additionally, setting clear goals and priorities can help navigate distractions by keeping your eyes on the proverbial prize.

In conclusion, maintaining focus amidst distractions requires a multifaceted approach that includes optimizing both external environments and internal states. By implementing strategic practices such as creating a conducive workspace, practicing mindfulness, utilizing effective time management techniques like the Pomodoro method, aligning tasks with peak energy times, and taking care of one's mental and physical health, individuals can significantly enhance their ability to stay focused in an increasingly distracting world. Embracing these strategies not only boosts productivity but also contributes to overall well-being.

References:

- Cirillo, F. (2006). The Pomodoro Technique. Retrieved from https://francescocirillo.com/pages/pomodoro-technique

- Kabat-Zinn, J. (1994). Wherever You Go, There You Are: Mindfulness Meditation in Everyday Life. Retrieved from https://www.mindfulnesscds.com/

- Mark, G., Gudith, D., & Klocke, U. (2008). The Cost of Interrupted Work: More Speed and Stress. Proceedings of the SIGCHI Conference on Human Factors in Computing Systems.

- National Sleep Foundation. (n.d.). How Much Sleep Do We Really Need? Retrieved from https://www.sleepfoundation.org/how-sleep-works/how-much-sleep-do-we-really-need

6

Real-Life Anecdotes from Men with ADHD

6.1 Stories of Struggle and Success

The journey of men with ADHD is often marked by a series of struggles and triumphs, each story unique yet universally resonant among those navigating similar paths. This section delves into the heartrending yet ultimately inspiring anecdotes that underscore the resilience and potential for success inherent in individuals with ADHD. These narratives not only illuminate the challenges faced but also highlight the strategies and mindsets that have led to personal and professional achievements, offering hope and practical guidance to others.

One compelling narrative involves Alex, a software developer who spent years battling undiagnosed ADHD. His story exemplifies the common struggle with maintaining focus, meeting deadlines, and managing interpersonal relationships at work. However, Alex's turning point came with his diagnosis in his late twenties, which he describes as both a relief and a call to action. Through cognitive behavioral therapy (CBT), medication, and a supportive network, Alex transformed his approach to work and life. He now runs a successful tech startup, employing strategies such as time-blocking and mindfulness exercises to manage his symptoms effectively.

Another anecdote comes from Brian, who struggled academically due to his ADHD but found solace and success in art. Brian's story highlights the importance of discovering one's strengths and passions as a pathway to overcoming ADHD-related challenges. With encouragement from mentors, he pursued an education in graphic design, leveraging his hyperfocus ability—a common trait among individuals with ADHD—to excel in his field. Today, Brian is an acclaimed graphic designer whose work has been featured in major publications.

- The role of early diagnosis and tailored interventions in transforming struggles into successes.

- How personal interests and strengths can serve as powerful motivators for men with ADHD.

- The significance of support systems—be it through family, friends, or professionals—in fostering resilience.

In conclusion, these stories from men with ADHD are testament to the fact that while the disorder presents significant hurdles, it also offers unique perspectives that can lead to remarkable achievements when harnessed correctly. The key lies in understanding one's own version of ADHD, seeking appropriate help, embracing one's strengths, and persistently working towards personalized goals. These real-life anecdotes serve not only as evidence of what is possible but also provide tangible hope for those on their own journey with ADHD.

6.2 Lessons Learned on the Journey with ADHD

The journey through life with ADHD is fraught with challenges, but it is also rich in lessons that can profoundly shape one's approach to both personal and professional endeavors. Men who have navigated the turbulent waters of ADHD have gleaned insights that not only aid in managing their condition but also offer valuable perspectives on resilience, adaptability, and success. This section explores the key lessons learned by men with ADHD, shedding light on how these insights contribute to a deeper understanding of the disorder and strategies for thriving despite its obstacles.

One of the most critical lessons learned is the importance of self-acceptance. Many men describe a transformative shift in their lives when they moved from viewing their ADHD as a debilitating flaw to seeing it as a facet of their identity that, while challenging, also confers unique strengths. This acceptance often marks the beginning of a more positive relationship with themselves and opens up new avenues for managing symptoms more effectively.

- The value of structured routines and organization cannot be overstated for individuals with ADHD. Learning to implement systems that accommodate impulsivity and distractibility has been crucial for many men in achieving their goals.

- Discovering personal passions and leveraging hyperfocus has led some to remarkable achievements in areas they are deeply passionate about. This intense focus, often seen as a hallmark of ADHD, can be an asset when directed towards productive activities.

- The role of support networks emerges as a recurring theme in these narratives. Whether it's family, friends, or professionals specialized in ADHD management, having a robust support system has been instrumental in navigating the complexities of life with ADHD.

In essence, these lessons underscore the multifaceted nature of living with ADHD. They highlight not just coping mechanisms but also underscore the potential for growth and achievement inherent in this journey. By embracing their unique neurodiversity, seeking appropriate support, and finding strategies that resonate with their individual experiences, men with ADHD demonstrate that it is possible to lead fulfilling lives marked by personal and professional successes.

6.3 Inspiring Others Through Personal Experiences

The power of personal stories in inspiring others cannot be overstated, especially when it comes to navigating the complexities of life with ADHD. Men who have lived through the ups and downs of ADHD possess a wealth of experiences that can illuminate the path for others facing similar challenges. This section delves into how sharing these personal journeys not only fosters a sense of community and understanding but also serves as a beacon of hope and motivation for individuals struggling to find their way.

One significant aspect of sharing personal experiences is the demystification of ADHD. By openly discussing their struggles, successes, and strategies for managing symptoms, men with ADHD help to break down the stigma associated with the condition. This openness encourages others to seek help, embrace their neurodiversity, and understand that having ADHD does not define one's potential for success.

- Personal anecdotes often highlight the importance of self-awareness in managing ADHD. Hearing how others have navigated self-discovery and acceptance can inspire individuals to embark on their own journey towards understanding and embracing their unique strengths.

- Stories of overcoming obstacles related to ADHD can motivate others to persevere through their challenges. Learning about someone who has achieved personal or professional success despite the hurdles posed by ADHD can provide a much-needed boost of confidence.

- The role of innovative coping strategies shared by those with lived experience is invaluable. These practical insights offer fresh perspectives on managing daily tasks, improving focus, and enhancing overall well-being.

In essence, inspiring others through personal experiences creates a ripple effect that extends far beyond individual achievements. It builds a supportive community where knowledge, empathy, and encouragement flow freely. Men who share their stories become role models, showing that while the journey with ADHD may be fraught with difficulties, it is also filled with opportunities for growth, achievement, and profound personal transformation.

References:

- Hallowell, E.M., & Ratey, J.J. (2011). Driven to Distraction (Revised): Recognizing and Coping with Attention Deficit Disorder. Anchor Books. This book provides insights into ADHD from two doctors who have the condition themselves, offering personal stories alongside professional advice.

- Brown, T.E. (2005). Attention Deficit Disorder: The Unfocused Mind in Children and Adults. Yale University Press. Brown discusses the complexities of ADHD in both children and adults, using personal anecdotes to illustrate how individuals can thrive despite their challenges.

- Fowler, T. (2020). ADHD 2.0: New Science and Essential Strategies for Thriving with Distraction - from Childhood through Adulthood. Ballantine Books. This book highlights the latest research on ADHD and shares stories of success and coping strategies from those who live with the condition.

- Tuckman, A. (2009). More Attention, Less Deficit: Success Strategies for Adults with ADHD. Specialty Press/A.D.D. Warehouse. Tuckman combines practical advice with real-life examples to help adults with ADHD find strategies that work for them.

7

Navigating the Emotional Rollercoaster

7.1 Dealing with Frustration and Low Self-Worth

The journey through understanding and managing ADHD in adult men often brings to the forefront the emotional challenges of frustration and low self-worth. These feelings are not only common but also deeply impactful, affecting various facets of life from personal relationships to professional achievements. The significance of addressing these emotional hurdles lies in their potential to either hinder or propel one's progress towards a fulfilling life despite ADHD.

Frustration in men with ADHD can stem from repeated experiences of misunderstanding, underachievement, or the constant struggle to meet societal expectations. This chronic frustration can erode self-confidence, leading to a diminished sense of self-worth. Unlike temporary setbacks that everyone faces, for men with ADHD, these feelings can be pervasive and persistent, coloring their view of themselves and their abilities.

To combat these challenges, it is crucial to adopt strategies that acknowledge and address both the symptoms of ADHD and their emotional consequences. One effective approach is cognitive-behavioral therapy (CBT), which helps individuals reframe negative thought patterns about themselves and develop more constructive responses to challenging situations. Additionally, mindfulness practices can aid in reducing impulsivity and increasing emotional regulation, offering a buffer against the immediate reactions of frustration.

In conclusion, dealing with frustration and low self-worth requires a multifaceted approach that includes psychological strategies, practical adjustments in daily living, and fostering an environment of support and understanding. By addressing these emotional aspects head-on, men with ADHD can navigate their condition more effectively, leading to improved well-being and life satisfaction.

- Building a support network: Surrounding oneself with understanding friends, family members, or joining support groups for people with ADHD can provide a sense of belonging and acceptance.

- Setting realistic goals: By breaking down larger objectives into manageable tasks, individuals can achieve small victories that bolster self-esteem over time.

- Focusing on strengths: Men with ADHD often possess unique talents such as creativity, problem-solving skills, or hyperfocus ability under certain conditions. Recognizing and leveraging these strengths can shift the focus from limitations to capabilities.

7.2 Overcoming Social Stigma

Overcoming social stigma is a critical aspect of navigating the emotional rollercoaster for adult men with ADHD. The societal misconceptions and prejudices surrounding ADHD can exacerbate feelings of isolation, shame, and low self-esteem. This section delves into strategies and insights aimed at dismantling the barriers erected by social stigma, facilitating a path towards acceptance and empowerment.

Social stigma often manifests through stereotypes and negative perceptions, which can lead to discrimination or exclusion in various spheres of life including work, education, and personal relationships. For men with ADHD, this stigma can compound the challenges they already face, making it harder to seek help or achieve their full potential. However, overcoming this stigma is possible through education, advocacy, and community support.

- Educating oneself and others: Knowledge is a powerful tool against ignorance. Understanding the facts about ADHD allows individuals to challenge misconceptions when they encounter them. Sharing accurate information with friends, family, and colleagues can also shift perceptions on a wider scale.

- Seeking out role models: Finding public figures or peers who have navigated similar challenges successfully can provide inspiration and proof that overcoming obstacles is possible. These stories can also offer practical advice on managing symptoms and leveraging strengths.

- Building a supportive community: Connecting with others who understand the experience of living with

ADHD can reduce feelings of isolation. Support groups—whether online or in-person—offer spaces to share experiences, strategies for coping with stigma, and mutual encouragement.

In addition to these strategies, advocating for systemic change is crucial. This involves pushing for policies that accommodate neurodiversity in educational institutions and workplaces, as well as promoting inclusive practices within society at large. By challenging stigma at both personal and structural levels, individuals can contribute to a more understanding and accepting environment for everyone affected by ADHD.

In conclusion, while social stigma presents significant hurdles for men with ADHD, it is not insurmountable. Through education, advocacy, community support, and personal resilience, it is possible to overcome these barriers. Doing so not only benefits individuals but also contributes to broader societal change towards acceptance and inclusion of neurodiversity.

7.3 Building Resilience

Building resilience is a cornerstone in the journey of adult men with ADHD, enabling them to navigate the complexities of their condition with strength and adaptability. This section explores the multifaceted approach to fostering resilience, emphasizing its role as a buffer against the emotional turmoil often experienced by those living with ADHD. Resilience is not an innate trait but a skill that can be developed over time through intentional practices and strategies.

At its core, resilience involves the ability to bounce back from setbacks, adapt to change, and keep going in the face of adversity. For men with ADHD, this means developing strategies that help manage symptoms while also cultivating a mindset that views challenges as opportunities for growth. The process of building resilience can be broken down into several key components:

- Self-awareness: Understanding one's own ADHD symptoms and how they impact various aspects of life is crucial. This awareness allows individuals to identify specific areas where they need support and develop personalized coping strategies.

- Mindfulness and stress management: Practices such as mindfulness meditation have been shown to reduce symptoms of anxiety and depression, common comorbidities in adults with ADHD. Learning stress management techniques can also help mitigate the impact of ADHD on daily functioning.

- Positive relationships: Cultivating supportive relationships is essential for building resilience. These connections provide emotional support, practical assistance, and a sense of belonging that can buffer against feelings of isolation or misunderstanding commonly experienced by those with ADHD.

- Achievable goal setting: Setting realistic goals and breaking them down into manageable steps can foster a sense of accomplishment and progress. This practice helps counteract feelings of overwhelm or failure that may arise from unmet expectations or societal pressures.

In addition to these personal strategies, seeking professional support when needed is also a vital component of building resilience. Therapy, coaching, or joining support groups specifically for adults with

ADHD can offer guidance, accountability, and encouragement throughout this journey.

In conclusion, building resilience in adult men with ADHD requires a holistic approach that addresses both the psychological aspects of living with ADHD and practical strategies for managing its symptoms. By focusing on self-awareness, stress management, positive relationships, achievable goal setting, and seeking support when necessary, individuals can enhance their capacity to navigate life's challenges more effectively.

References:

- Barkley, R. A. (2015). Attention-Deficit Hyperactivity Disorder: A Handbook for Diagnosis and Treatment. Guilford Publications.

- National Institute of Mental Health. (2020). Attention-Deficit/Hyperactivity Disorder. https://www.nimh.nih.gov/health/topics/attention-deficit-hyperactivity-disorder-adhd

- Safren, S. A., Sprich, S., Perlman, C., & Otto, M. W. (2005). Mastering Your Adult ADHD: A Cognitive-

Behavioral Treatment Program Client Workbook. Oxford University Press.

- Zylowska, L. (2012). The Mindfulness Prescription for Adult ADHD: An 8-Step Program for Strengthening Attention, Managing Emotions, and Achieving Your Goals. Shambhala Publications.

8

Building Supportive Relationships

8.1 Improving Communication Skills

The ability to communicate effectively is crucial for everyone, but it holds particular significance for men with ADHD. This section delves into the nuances of enhancing communication skills, a vital component for building supportive relationships and navigating daily challenges. Effective communication not only aids in expressing thoughts and needs clearly but also plays a pivotal role in fostering understanding and empathy among peers, family members, and professional circles.

Men with ADHD often encounter hurdles in social interactions due to impulsivity, difficulty maintaining focus during conversations, or misinterpreting social cues. These challenges can lead to misunderstandings and strained relationships. However, by adopting specific strategies tailored to their unique needs, individuals can significantly improve their interpersonal communication skills.

Incorporating these strategies requires patience and practice. It may also be beneficial to seek support from therapists or counselors who specialize in ADHD to develop personalized approaches based on individual strengths and weaknesses. Over time, improving communication skills can lead to stronger relationships both professionally and personally, enhancing overall quality of life for men with ADHD.

Beyond personal efforts, creating an environment that fosters open dialogue about ADHD challenges can encourage empathy and understanding from others. By sharing experiences and strategies that have been effective in managing symptoms related to communication difficulties, individuals can contribute to a more supportive community that recognizes the value of diverse perspectives.

- Active Listening: This involves fully concentrating on the speaker, understanding their message, responding thoughtfully, and remembering the discussion. It's essential for men with ADHD to practice mindfulness during conversations to enhance their active listening capabilities.

- Non-Verbal Communication: Understanding and using non-verbal cues effectively—such as eye contact, facial expressions, and body language—can greatly improve how messages are received and interpreted by others.

- Clear and Concise Messaging: Given the tendency towards distractibility, it's beneficial for individuals with ADHD to practice articulating their thoughts in a clear and concise manner. This helps in minimizing misunderstandings.

- Pause Before Responding: Taking a moment to process information before replying can help in formulating more thoughtful responses and reduce impulsivity in conversations.

- Feedback Loops: Encouraging open feedback about one's communication style can provide valuable insights into areas of improvement. Constructive criticism should be seen as an opportunity for growth rather than criticism.

8.2 Finding Professional Help When Needed

Finding professional help when needed is a critical step for individuals, especially men with ADHD, in building supportive relationships and managing the challenges that come with the condition. This section explores the importance of seeking professional assistance, the types of professionals available, and strategies to find the right support system.

Recognizing when to seek professional help is often the first hurdle. Many men with ADHD might delay or avoid seeking help due to stigma, fear of judgment, or simply not recognizing that their struggles could be mitigated with professional intervention. It's crucial to understand that seeking help is a sign of strength and an important step towards improving one's quality of life.

- Identifying the Need: Understanding specific challenges related to ADHD, such as difficulty in maintaining relationships, managing emotions, or staying organized at work can indicate when professional help might be beneficial.

- Types of Professionals: Psychologists, psychiatrists, and specialized ADHD coaches are among the professionals who can offer support. Each brings different expertise—psychologists and psychiatrists can diagnose and treat ADHD through therapy and medication, while ADHD coaches offer strategies for daily management without providing medical treatment.

- Finding the Right Fit: It's essential to find a professional who has experience with adult ADHD. Recommendations from trusted healthcare providers or local ADHD support groups can be invaluable in this process.

- Making Use of Online Resources: Numerous online directories and resources are dedicated to helping individuals connect with mental health professionals experienced in treating ADHD. These platforms often allow users to filter searches by location, specialty, and insurance acceptance.

  Beyond individual efforts in finding professional help, creating an environment that encourages open discussion about mental health challenges is vital. Sharing experiences about seeking professional assistance can demystify the process for others and foster a supportive community atmosphere. Ultimately, finding the right professional help when needed not only aids in managing ADHD symptoms but also enhances overall well-being by supporting personal growth and stronger relationships.

In conclusion, while navigating the journey to find appropriate professional help may seem daunting at first, understanding one's needs and knowing how to access resources can make this process significantly more manageable. With patience and persistence, finding a supportive professional ally is within reach for those willing to take this important step.

8.3 Creating a Supportive Environment

The essence of creating a supportive environment lies in fostering a space—whether at home, work, or within social circles—that actively promotes understanding, acceptance, and encouragement for individuals with ADHD. This nurturing atmosphere is pivotal not only for the person with ADHD but also for those around them, enhancing mutual respect and empathy. The transition from seeking professional help to cultivating an inclusive environment marks a significant step towards sustainable support and personal growth.

Creating such an environment involves several key strategies that collectively contribute to a more supportive setting. Firstly, education plays a crucial role. Informing family members, friends, and colleagues about the nuances of ADHD can dismantle myths and reduce stigma associated with the condition. Knowledge empowers people to offer appropriate support and make accommodations that can significantly ease daily challenges faced by those with ADHD.

- Implementing structured routines helps in minimizing distractions and creating predictability, which can be particularly beneficial for individuals struggling with organization due to ADHD.

- Encouraging open communication fosters an atmosphere where feelings and experiences related to ADHD can be shared without fear of judgment. This openness is vital for emotional support and understanding.

- Adapting physical spaces to reduce overstimulation—such as organizing cluttered areas or using noise-cancelling headphones in noisy environments—can make environments more conducive to focus and relaxation for someone with ADHD.

Beyond these practical steps, promoting inclusivity through empathy is fundamental. Recognizing that each individual's experience with ADHD is unique ensures that support is tailored and meaningful. Celebrating small victories together reinforces positive behavior changes and boosts self-esteem.

In conclusion, creating a supportive environment for individuals with ADHD requires concerted efforts across multiple fronts—from educating oneself and others about the condition to making thoughtful adjustments in daily routines and communication styles. By doing so, we not only aid in managing the symptoms of ADHD but also contribute to building stronger, more empathetic relationships that enrich everyone involved.

References:

- CHADD (Children and Adults with Attention-Deficit/Hyperactivity Disorder) provides comprehensive information on ADHD, including strategies for creating supportive environments at home and work. Visit www.chadd.org.

- The Attention Deficit Disorder Association (ADDA) offers resources and tips for adults with ADHD to improve their living spaces and routines. Check out www.add.org.

- Understood.org features articles and guides on how to foster inclusive environments for children and adults with learning and attention issues, including ADHD. See more at www.understood.org.

- The National Institute of Mental Health (NIMH) provides scientific information on ADHD, covering symptoms, treatments, and recommendations for supporting individuals with the disorder. Their website is www.nimh.nih.gov.

9

For Partners, Family Members, Friends, and Employers

9.1 Understanding ADHD in Adult Men

The exploration of ADHD in adult men is crucial for a comprehensive understanding of how this condition manifests uniquely across different genders. This section delves into the nuances of ADHD specifically in adult males, highlighting the importance of recognizing and addressing these distinctions to foster better support systems and management strategies.

ADHD in men often goes undiagnosed or misdiagnosed due to societal expectations and stereotypes about masculinity. Men are frequently expected to be self-reliant, stoic, and in control of their emotions and actions. These cultural norms can mask symptoms of ADHD, leading many to struggle silently without understanding the root cause of their challenges. The hyperactivity aspect, which is more commonly associated with childhood ADHD, may present differently in adults as restlessness or an internal sense of agitation rather than overt physical activity.

Inattention, another core symptom of ADHD, can significantly impact an adult man's life by affecting his ability to stay organized, meet deadlines, and maintain focus on tasks at work or home. This can lead to feelings of frustration, low self-esteem, and underachievement. Moreover, impulsivity may manifest through risky behaviors or quick decision-making without considering the consequences, further complicating personal and professional relationships.

This section underscores the significance of personalized approaches when dealing with ADHD in adult men. By acknowledging the unique challenges they face and offering targeted solutionsâ€"ranging from behavioral strategies to lifestyle adjustmentsâ€"we can empower men with ADHD to lead more fulfilling lives. Additionally, fostering open conversations around mental health within male communities can help break down stigmas and encourage more men to seek help when needed.

- Understanding the neurological basis behind ADHD helps in demystifying why certain behaviors occur. It's not a lack of willpower but rather differences in brain function that affect attention regulation and impulse control.

- Strategies tailored specifically for men with ADHD include leveraging technology for organization, engaging in regular physical activity to reduce restlessness, and seeking careers that offer flexibility or match their high energy levels.

- Emotional regulation is another critical area where men with ADHD may need support. Developing coping mechanisms for frustration and disappointment can help mitigate the emotional rollercoaster often experienced by those with ADHD.

9.2 How to Offer Support

Offering support to someone with ADHD, especially adult men who might face unique societal pressures and expectations, requires a nuanced understanding of the condition and a compassionate approach. This section delves into practical ways family members, friends, employers, and partners can provide meaningful support that acknowledges the challenges while empowering individuals with ADHD.

Firstly, it's essential to recognize that support goes beyond mere acknowledgment of the condition. It involves active engagement in learning about ADHD's manifestations and impacts. For those close to an adult man with ADHD, this means understanding how symptoms like inattention, hyperactivity, and impulsivity uniquely affect him in his daily life and relationships.

- Creating an environment that reduces distractions can be incredibly beneficial for someone struggling with inattention. This might mean establishing quiet workspaces at home or offering flexible working arrangements for employees with ADHD.

- Encouraging regular physical activity is another supportive strategy. Exercise not only helps in managing restlessness but also improves overall brain function, which can mitigate some of the cognitive challenges associated with ADHD.

- Implementing organizational tools and strategies together can also offer substantial support. Whether it's using digital apps for scheduling and reminders or setting up structured routines at home or work, these strategies can help manage forgetfulness and procrastination.

   Beyond practical adjustments, emotional support plays a critical role in supporting an adult man with ADHD. It's important to foster open communication where feelings of frustration or inadequacy can be expressed without judgment. Validating their experiences rather than minimizing them encourages individuals to share their struggles openly.

- Promoting professional help when necessary is also crucial. Encouraging visits to therapists or counselors who specialize in ADHD can provide them with coping mechanisms tailored to their specific needs.

- Lastly, celebrating successes—no matter how small—can boost self-esteem and motivation. Acknowledging progress helps reinforce positive behaviors and reminds individuals that their efforts are recognized and appreciated.

In conclusion, offering support to men with ADHD involves a combination of practical strategies tailored to their unique challenges and fostering an environment of emotional safety and encouragement. By adopting these approaches, partners, family members, friends, and employers can significantly contribute to the well-being and success of men managing ADHD.

9.3 Encouraging Constructive Dialogue

Encouraging constructive dialogue is a pivotal aspect of supporting individuals with ADHD, particularly adult men who may face societal pressures that discourage open emotional expression. This section explores the importance of fostering an environment where constructive dialogue can flourish, offering insights into techniques and approaches that facilitate effective communication.

Constructive dialogue involves more than just talking; it's about creating a space where individuals feel safe to express their thoughts, feelings, and experiences without fear of judgment or dismissal. For partners, family members, friends, and employers, this means actively listening and responding in a way that validates the individual's experiences. It's crucial to approach conversations with empathy, understanding that ADHD affects everyone differently and what works for one person may not work for another.

- Begin by setting aside dedicated time for discussions, ensuring there are no distractions. This signals that you are fully present and value the conversation.

- Use open-ended questions to encourage deeper reflection and sharing. Questions like "How did you feel about that?" or "What can we do together to improve this situation?" invite meaningful responses.

- Acknowledge feelings before jumping to solutions. Sometimes, the act of being heard is more important than immediately fixing a problem.

- Practice active listening by summarizing what the other person has said and asking if you've understood them correctly. This demonstrates your engagement and helps clarify any misunderstandings on the spot.

In addition to these strategies, it's essential to recognize when professional help might be beneficial. Encouraging someone to seek therapy or counseling should be done sensitively, emphasizing that seeking help is a sign of strength and an important step towards managing ADHD effectively.

Celebrating successes plays a significant role in encouraging constructive dialogue as well. Recognizing achievements—no matter how small—can boost confidence and motivate further progress. It reinforces the idea that efforts are seen and appreciated, fostering a positive atmosphere for future conversations.

In conclusion, encouraging constructive dialogue is not just about facilitating better communication; it's about building trust, understanding, and mutual respect. By adopting these approaches, those close to individuals with ADHD can significantly enhance their support system, contributing positively to their loved one's journey through managing ADHD.

References:

- Barkley, R.A. (2015). Attention-Deficit Hyperactivity Disorder: A Handbook for Diagnosis and Treatment. Guilford Press.

- Murphy, K., & Barkley, R.A. (1996). Attention Deficit Hyperactivity Disorder Adults: Clinician's Guide. Academic Press.

- Nadeau, K.G., Littman, E.B., & Quinn, P.O. (Eds.). (2015). Understanding Women with AD/HD. Advantage Books.

- Ramsay, J.R. (2020). Rethinking Adult ADHD: Helping Clients Turn Intentions into Actions. American Psychological Association.

- Tuckman, A. (2009). More Attention, Less Deficit: Success Strategies for Adults with ADHD. Specialty Press/A.D.D. Warehouse.

10

Thriving with ADHD in the Modern World

10.1 Redefining the Relationship with ADHD

The journey of understanding and living with ADHD, especially for adult men, necessitates a profound shift in perspective—a redefinition of one's relationship with ADHD. This reevaluation is not merely about coping strategies or symptom management but involves embracing ADHD as an integral part of one's identity that comes with its unique strengths and challenges.

Traditionally, ADHD has been viewed through a deficit-focused lens, emphasizing the difficulties it presents in daily functioning, particularly in societal structures like traditional work environments or educational systems not designed for neurodivergent minds. However, a transformative approach begins with recognizing and valuing the positive aspects and potential advantages of ADHD traits, such as creativity, hyperfocus on passionate interests, resilience, and the ability to think outside conventional frameworks.

This redefined relationship involves moving away from stigma and self-criticism towards acceptance and self-compassion. It requires an understanding that while ADHD can present significant hurdles, it also bestows unique gifts. For many men, this realization fosters a sense of liberation and empowerment. They learn to navigate their lives by leveraging their strengths rather than being solely fixated on mitigating weaknesses.

In conclusion, redefining the relationship with ADHD is about shifting from viewing it as a disorder to be battled against to seeing it as a unique aspect of one's identity that offers both challenges and opportunities. By focusing on strengths, seeking supportive communities that understand neurodiversity, and employing tailored strategies for managing symptoms, individuals can transform their experience with ADHD from surviving to thriving.

- Embracing Neurodiversity: Recognizing that ADHD is a part of the broader spectrum of neurodiversity which includes a range of neurological variations such as autism spectrum disorder (ASD), dyslexia, and more. This perspective promotes acceptance and appreciation of different brain makeups.

- Personalized Strategies: Developing personalized coping strategies that align with individual strengths and interests rather than adopting a one-size-fits-all approach. This might include choosing careers or hobbies that capitalize on hyperfocus abilities or creative thinking.

- Mindfulness Practices: Incorporating mindfulness practices into daily routines to improve focus, reduce impulsivity, and manage stress—key areas often affected by ADHD.

10.2 Strategies for Success in Work and Life

The journey towards thriving with ADHD in the modern world involves not only a redefinition of one's relationship with ADHD but also the implementation of practical strategies for success in both professional and personal spheres. This section delves into how individuals with ADHD can harness their unique strengths to achieve fulfillment and success, navigating through challenges with resilience and creativity.

One pivotal aspect of finding success is the cultivation of an environment that aligns with ADHD strengths. For many, this means seeking out dynamic, fast-paced work settings where quick thinking and adaptability are valued over conventional organizational skills. Careers in entrepreneurship, creative arts, or technology often provide the flexibility and stimulation that individuals with ADHD crave and excel in.

Moreover, leveraging technology can play a crucial role in managing daily tasks and responsibilities. Digital tools like task management apps or timers can help counteract tendencies towards forgetfulness or time mismanagement. These tools act as external memory aids, enabling individuals to focus on their strengths rather than being bogged down by logistical details.

- Creating structured routines: Establishing predictable patterns for work and leisure can help mitigate feelings of overwhelm and assist in prioritizing tasks effectively.

- Building a supportive network: Surrounding oneself with understanding peers, mentors, or professionals who recognize the value of neurodiversity can provide both emotional support and practical advice tailored to navigating life with ADHD.

- Continuous learning: Engaging in lifelong learning about ADHD, including staying informed about new research or coping strategies, empowers individuals to make informed decisions about their care and lifestyle choices.

In addition to these strategies, it's essential for individuals to advocate for themselves in the workplace. This might involve requesting reasonable accommodations under laws designed to protect those with disabilities or simply initiating open conversations about one's needs and strengths with employers. Self-advocacy fosters a more inclusive environment that recognizes diverse talents while accommodating different ways of achieving objectives.

Ultimately, thriving with ADHD requires a multifaceted approach that combines self-awareness, strategic planning, and proactive engagement with one's environment. By focusing on their inherent strengths while employing targeted strategies to navigate challenges, individuals with ADHD can unlock their full potential in both their personal lives and careers.

10.3 Empowerment through Education

The empowerment of individuals with ADHD through education is a cornerstone in the journey towards thriving in today's fast-paced world. This section explores how targeted educational strategies and informed learning environments can significantly enhance the lives of those with ADHD, fostering a sense of empowerment that transcends academic achievements to impact all areas of life.

Education for individuals with ADHD goes beyond traditional learning methods. It involves understanding the unique ways in which they process information and tailoring teaching methods to accommodate these differences. For instance, interactive learning that incorporates physical movement can be more effective than conventional lecture-based approaches. This adaptive strategy not only caters to their need for engagement but also capitalizes on their ability to think outside the box, turning potential obstacles into assets.

Moreover, empowerment through education is not limited to formal schooling. It encompasses a broad spectrum of learning opportunities, including vocational training, online courses, workshops, and seminars specifically designed or adapted for those with ADHD. These platforms offer practical skills and knowledge that can be directly applied to workplace scenarios, enhancing employability and career progression.

- Personalized Learning Plans: Developing individualized education programs (IEPs) or 504 plans that are tailored to each student's specific needs, strengths, and interests.

- Technology Integration: Utilizing technology in the classroom to provide alternative ways of learning and demonstrating knowledge. Apps and software designed for time management, organization, and study skills can be particularly beneficial.

- Mentorship Programs: Connecting students with ADHD with mentors who either have ADHD themselves or are trained in supporting students with ADHD can provide valuable guidance, encouragement, and understanding.

In addition to adapting educational practices, fostering an environment of acceptance and understanding within educational institutions is crucial. Educators and peers who recognize the strengths that come with neurodiversity contribute significantly to creating a supportive learning atmosphere. This positive reinforcement helps individuals with ADHD develop confidence in their abilities while navigating their educational journey.

Ultimately, empowerment through education for those with ADHD is about more than just academic success; it's about equipping them with the tools, strategies, and confidence needed to excel in all facets of life. By embracing innovative educational approaches and fostering inclusive environments, we can unlock the vast potential residing within individuals with ADHD.

References:

- DuPaul, G.J., & Stoner, G. (2014). ADHD in the Schools: Assessment and Intervention Strategies. Guilford Press.

- Murphy, K.R., & Barkley, R.A. (1996). Attention Deficit Hyperactivity Disorder: A Clinical Workbook. The Guilford Press.

- Rief, S.F. (2005). How to Reach and Teach Children with ADD/ADHD: Practical Techniques, Strategies, and Interventions. Jossey-Bass.

- Barkley, R.A. (2015). Attention-Deficit Hyperactivity Disorder: A Handbook for Diagnosis and Treatment. Guilford Press.

- National Resource Center on ADHD. (n.d.). Educational Rights for Children with ADHD in Public Schools. Retrieved from https://chadd.org/for-parents/educational-rights-for-children-with-adhd-in-public-schools/

11

Additional Resources for Further Exploration

1.1 Books, Websites, and Communities

The exploration of resources such as books, websites, and communities plays a pivotal role in understanding and managing ADHD in adult men. These resources offer a wealth of knowledge, practical advice, and support that can significantly enhance the journey towards effective management of ADHD. They serve not only as tools for education but also as platforms for connection and empowerment among those affected by ADHD.

Books like "ADHD in Adult Men - Hyperactivity In Adults Survival Guide" provide comprehensive insights into the condition, debunking myths and offering strategies for overcoming the challenges it presents. However, the landscape of literature on this topic is vast and varied, encompassing both academic research and personal narratives that together enrich an individual's understanding of ADHD.

- Websites are invaluable for staying updated with the latest research, finding tips for daily management of symptoms, and accessing online assessments. Sites such as ADDitude Magazine offer articles written by healthcare professionals and individuals with ADHD alike, creating a balanced perspective on living with ADHD.

- Communities, both online and offline, provide a sense of belonging and support that is crucial for individuals navigating the complexities of ADHD. Online forums like Reddit's r/ADHD foster anonymous discussions where individuals can share experiences and strategies without fear of judgment. Local support groups offer face-to-face interactions that can lead to lasting friendships and networks of support.

  In addition to these resources, podcasts hosted by experts in the field or individuals who have ADHD themselves can be an engaging way to receive information and feel connected to a larger community.

They often feature interviews with professionals or discuss specific aspects of living with ADHD in depth.

Ultimately, books, websites, and communities dedicated to ADHD in adult men are more than just sources of information; they are lifelines that connect individuals to solutions, support systems, and each other. By leveraging these resources effectively, men with ADHD can navigate their challenges more successfully and lead fulfilling lives despite the hurdles posed by their condition.

1.1 Professional Organizations and Support Groups

The significance of professional organizations and support groups in the context of ADHD in adult men cannot be overstated. These entities play a crucial role not only in providing access to the latest research and treatment modalities but also in offering a platform for individuals to share experiences, strategies, and encouragement. This dual function helps bridge the gap between clinical knowledge and lived experience, fostering a more comprehensive approach to managing ADHD.

Professional organizations such as the Attention Deficit Disorder Association (ADDA) and Children and Adults with Attention-Deficit/Hyperactivity Disorder (CHADD) are at the forefront of ADHD advocacy, research, and education. They offer a plethora of resources including webinars, conferences, publications, and directories of ADHD professionals. These resources are invaluable for both individuals with ADHD and their families, as well as clinicians seeking to enhance their practice.

- Webinars and Conferences: These events provide opportunities for learning about cutting-edge research, treatment innovations, and management strategies from leading experts in the field.

- Publications: Journals, newsletters, and online articles disseminate current findings on ADHD diagnosis, treatment options, coping mechanisms, and more.

- Directories of Professionals: Access to vetted lists of healthcare providers who specialize in ADHD can significantly ease the process of finding supportive medical care.

Support groups offer another layer of assistance by facilitating connections among individuals facing similar challenges. Whether through online forums or local meetups, these groups create safe spaces for sharing personal stories, exchanging practical advice on navigating daily life with ADHD, and offering emotional support. The collective wisdom found within these communities can often lead to breakthroughs in personal management strategies that might not be discovered through traditional medical consultations alone.

In essence, professional organizations and support groups serve as vital components of a holistic approach to managing ADHD in adult men. By leveraging these resources effectively, individuals can gain deeper insights into their condition while feeling supported by a community that understands their unique struggles. This combination of expert knowledge and peer support is instrumental in empowering men with ADHD to lead more structured lives filled with greater achievements despite the hurdles posed by their condition.

1.11 Technology Tools for Managing Symptoms

The advent of technology has brought about a significant shift in how individuals with ADHD manage their symptoms. Beyond traditional treatment modalities, such as medication and therapy, technology tools have emerged as a vital component in the arsenal against ADHD, especially for adult men seeking innovative ways to cope with their condition. This section delves into the various technological tools designed to assist in symptom management, highlighting their importance and utility.

Smartphone applications are at the forefront of this technological revolution. Apps specifically designed for ADHD can help users organize their tasks, set reminders for medications and appointments, and even provide platforms for mindfulness and stress management. These apps often incorporate gamification elements to make daily task management more engaging. For instance, habit-tracking apps reward users for completing tasks or maintaining routines, which can be particularly beneficial for those struggling with procrastination or forgetfulness.

- Task Management Apps: These apps help users break down projects into manageable tasks, set deadlines, and prioritize work effectively.

- Reminder Systems: Built-in notification features serve as cues to take medication or prepare for upcoming appointments.

- Mindfulness and Meditation Apps: Offering guided sessions to reduce anxiety and improve focus, these tools are invaluable for daily mental health maintenance.

In addition to smartphone applications, wearable technology has also gained traction as a means of managing ADHD symptoms. Devices like smartwatches can monitor physiological responses such as heart rate variability (HRV), which may indicate stress levels or emotional dysregulation common among adults with ADHD. By alerting wearers to changes in their physiological state, these devices encourage proactive strategies to address potential triggers before they escalate into more significant issues.

Furthermore, online platforms that offer cognitive behavioral therapy (CBT) exercises have become increasingly accessible. These platforms provide structured programs that users can follow at their own pace to develop coping strategies and cognitive restructuring techniques aimed at reducing negative thought patterns associated with ADHD.

The integration of technology into symptom management represents a paradigm shift towards personalized care tailored to the unique needs of individuals with ADHD. By leveraging these tools effectively, adult men can gain greater control over their symptoms, leading to improved productivity and overall quality of life despite the challenges posed by ADHD.

References:

- Gustafson, D. H., McTavish, F. M., Chih, M. Y., Atwood, A. K., Johnson, R. A., Boyle, M. G., Levy, M. S., Driscoll, H., Chisholm, S. M., Dillenburg, L., Isham, A., & Shah, D. (2014). A smartphone application to support recovery from alcoholism: a randomized clinical trial. JAMA Psychiatry.

- Kollins, S. H., DeLoss, D. J., Cañadas, E., Lutz, J., Findling, R. L., Keefe, R. S.E., Epstein,J.N.& Cutler,A.J.(2020).A novel digital intervention for actively reducing severity of paediatric ADHD (STARS-ADHD): a randomised controlled trial.Lancet Psychiatry.

- Ruscio,A.M.,Hallion,L.S.&Lim,C.C.W.(2017).Cognitive-behavioral therapy for mental disorders.Psychiatry Research.

- Saarinen,A.I,Park,S.&Kangasniemi,M.(2019).Use of wearable devices and social media to improve physical activity and dietary behaviors among college students: A systematic review.International Journal of Environmental Research and Public Health.

12

Overcoming Challenges in Daily Life with ADHD

12.1 Strategies for Managing Time and Priorities

The challenge of managing time and priorities is particularly acute for men with ADHD, who often struggle with procrastination, forgetfulness, and underestimating the time required for tasks. This section delves into effective strategies tailored to address these issues, enabling individuals to navigate their daily lives more efficiently.

Understanding the unique ways in which ADHD affects time management and prioritization is crucial. Men with ADHD might find themselves easily distracted, leading to difficulty in completing tasks or following through on commitments. The first step towards improvement involves acknowledging these challenges without judgment, adopting a compassionate approach towards oneself.

Incorporating these strategies requires patience and practice. It's important to celebrate small victories along the way and adjust techniques as needed based on what works best for an individual's lifestyle and preferences. Over time, these approaches can lead to significant improvements in managing time and priorities effectively despite the challenges posed by ADHD.

- Use of Technology: Leveraging technology can be a game-changer. Apps that focus on task management and reminders can help keep track of deadlines and appointments. Digital calendars are particularly useful for visualizing how one's time is allocated throughout the day or week.

- Breaking Down Tasks: Large projects can seem overwhelming, leading to avoidance or procrastination. Breaking down tasks into smaller, manageable steps can make them seem more achievable and less daunting. This also provides a clear roadmap of what needs to be done, making it easier to start.

- Prioritization Techniques: Not all tasks are created equal; some are more urgent or important than others. Techniques such as the Eisenhower Matrix can help men with ADHD distinguish between tasks that need immediate attention and those that can wait. This helps in focusing efforts where they are most needed.
- Time Blocking: Allocating specific blocks of time to different activities can help in managing distractions and maintaining focus. This technique ensures that there's a designated time for work, leisure, and rest, reducing the likelihood of overcommitting or neglecting personal needs.

12.2 Organization Techniques for Adults with ADHD

For adults living with ADHD, mastering organization can often feel like navigating a labyrinth without a map. The inherent challenges of ADHD, such as impulsivity, distractibility, and difficulty in maintaining focus, can make traditional organizational strategies less effective. However, by tailoring organization techniques to their unique needs, adults with ADHD can transform their approach to organization from a source of frustration into a tool for empowerment.

The cornerstone of effective organization for adults with ADHD involves leveraging structure in a way that aligns with their cognitive patterns. This means creating systems that are flexible enough to accommodate the variability in attention and energy levels characteristic of ADHD while being robust enough to provide the necessary scaffolding to support daily functioning.

- Visual Organization Systems: Visual cues play a critical role in helping individuals with ADHD stay organized. Using color-coded systems for filing documents or scheduling tasks can provide immediate visual feedback that is easier to process than text alone. Similarly, large wall calendars or whiteboards can offer a big-picture view of upcoming responsibilities and deadlines, making it easier to plan and prioritize.
- Digital Tools: In an era where technology is ubiquitous, digital tools offer unprecedented support for organization. Apps designed specifically for task management can be particularly beneficial for adults with ADHD by providing customizable reminders and

allowing users to break down projects into more manageable sub-tasks. Moreover, many of these apps include features that encourage regular review and adjustment of tasks and priorities.

- Routine Building: Establishing routines can help automate recurring tasks, reducing the cognitive load required to initiate and complete them. For example, dedicating specific days or times for certain activities (e.g., Sunday evenings for planning the week ahead) can create predictable structures that make time management more intuitive.

- Decluttering Regularly: Physical clutter can be both a symptom and a cause of disorganization in individuals with ADHD. Implementing regular decluttering sessionsâ€"whether daily tidying up or weekly reviews of workspacesâ€"can prevent clutter from becoming overwhelming and reduce distractions.

Incorporating these techniques into daily life doesn't just improve external organization; it also fosters a sense of internal calmness and control. It's important for adults with ADHD to recognize that mastery over organization is not about perfection but about finding strategies that enhance functionality and well-being in their personal and professional lives. Experimentation and adaptation are key; what works well one month may need tweaking the next as demands and circumstances change. Celebrating successes, no matter how small, reinforces positive behaviors and motivates continued effort towards greater organizational competence.

12.3 Coping with Distractions and Maintaining Focus

For individuals with ADHD, the challenge of coping with distractions and maintaining focus is a daily struggle that can significantly impact their personal and professional lives. This section delves into strategies specifically designed to mitigate these challenges, offering new insights into creating an environment conducive to enhanced concentration and productivity.

The first step in addressing distractions is identifying their sources. Distractions can be external, such as noise or interruptions from others, or internal, like wandering thoughts or emotional disturbances. Recognizing the types of distractions most disruptive allows for targeted strategies to combat them effectively.

- Creating a Distraction-Free Environment: Tailoring one's physical workspace to minimize external distractions is crucial. This might involve using noise-cancelling headphones to block out ambient noise or setting up a dedicated work area away from high-traffic parts of the home or office.

- Utilizing Technology Wisely: While digital tools offer significant organizational benefits, they can also be sources of distraction. Employing website blockers during work hours or setting specific times to check emails and social media can help maintain focus on tasks at hand.

- Time Management Techniques: Techniques such as the Pomodoro Technique, which involves working for set periods followed by short breaks, can enhance focus by providing structure and regular intervals for rest. This method not only helps in maintaining concentration but also in managing energy levels throughout the day.

- Mindfulness and Stress Reduction Practices: Internal distractions often stem from stress or emotional turmoil. Incorporating mindfulness practices such as meditation or deep-breathing exercises into one's routine can improve overall mental clarity and reduce susceptibility to internal distractions.

Beyond these strategies, it's essential for individuals with ADHD to cultivate self-compassion and realistic expectations about their productivity levels. Understanding that some days will be more productive than others helps in maintaining motivation and resilience in the face of ongoing challenges with focus and distractibility.

In conclusion, while coping with distractions and maintaining focus presents significant hurdles for those with ADHD, employing tailored strategies that address both external and internal sources of distraction can lead to improved concentration and productivity. Experimentation with different techniques is key; what works well for one individual may not be as effective for another. The goal is not perfection but progress towards greater control over one's attentional resources.

References:

- Barkley, R. A. (2015). Attention-Deficit Hyperactivity Disorder: A Handbook for Diagnosis and Treatment. Guilford Publications. This handbook provides comprehensive information on ADHD, including strategies for managing distractions.

- Kabat-Zinn, J. (1994). Wherever You Go, There You Are: Mindfulness Meditation in Everyday Life. Hyperion. Kabat-Zinn's work introduces mindfulness meditation as a practice for improving focus and reducing stress.

- Cirillo, F. (2006). The Pomodoro Technique (The Pomodoro). LuLu.com. This book outlines the Pomodoro Technique, a time management method beneficial for maintaining focus and productivity.

- Hallowell, E. M., & Ratey, J. J. (2011). Driven to Distraction (Revised): Recognizing and Coping with Attention Deficit Disorder. Anchor Books. This revised edition offers insights into coping strategies specifically tailored for individuals with ADHD.

"ADHD in Adult Men - Hyperactivity In Adults Survival Guide" is an enlightening non-fiction work that delves into the complexities of Attention Deficit Hyperactivity Disorder (ADHD) as it specifically affects adult men. This book serves as a comprehensive resource, debunking prevalent myths and providing a deep understanding of ADHD's neurological basis and its distinct impact on men. It covers how ADHD influences various life areas, including professional environments, personal relationships, and self-esteem.

The guide adopts a holistic approach to managing ADHD symptoms, incorporating not just medication but also dietary recommendations, exercise plans, cognitive behavioral strategies, and mindfulness practices tailored for men dealing with hyperactivity and attention difficulties. It emphasizes the importance of self-acceptance and leveraging personal strengths to tackle challenges head-on.

A crucial component of this book is its practical survival toolkit, which offers time management techniques, organizational tips, and strategies for maintaining focus amidst distractions. The inclusion of real-life stories from men who have navigated life with ADHD adds a relatable and motivational aspect to the narrative. Additionally, the guide tackles the emotional challenges associated with ADHD, such as frustration, low self-worth, and social stigma. It provides advice on fostering supportive relationships and effective communication skills while also guiding readers toward seeking professional assistance when necessary.

Furthermore, "ADHD in Adult Men" extends its utility to those around men with ADHD—partners, family members, friends, and employers—by fostering empathy and promoting constructive conversations about this often-misunderstood condition. This book is not only about surviving with ADHD but thriving despite it. It empowers readers to redefine their relationship with ADHD and pursue fulfilling lives through education and empowerment.

www.ingramcontent.com/pod-product-compliance
Lightning Source LLC
LaVergne TN
LVHW020006240225
804377LV00012B/1247